ABOVE ALL

HE TOOK *the* FALL *and* THOUGHT *of* ME...

ABOVE ALL

BRENNAN MANNING

AUTHOR *of* THE RAGAMUFFIN GOSPEL

FOREWORD BY

MICHAEL W. SMITH

Published in association with the literary agency of Alive Communications, Inc.,
7680 Goddard Street, Suite 200, Colorado Springs, Colorado 80920.

Cover and Interior Design: The Office of Bill Chiaravalle / www.officeofbc.com

---

Library of Congress Cataloging-in-Publication Data

Manning, Brennan.
    Above all / by Brennan Manning.
        p. cm.
    ISBN 1-59145-052-7
    1. Jesus Christ—Person and offices. I. Title.

BT203 .M33 2003
232—dc21

2002038832

Printed in the United States of America
03 04 05 06 07 BVG 9 8 7 6 5 4 3 2 1

For my stepdaughters,
Simone and Nicole, who for the
last twenty years have loved me in my brokenness.

ACKNOWLEDGMENTS

I would like to express my heartfelt gratitude to
Joey Paul, for asking me to write this book; to Jennifer Stair,
for her careful and cohesive editing; and to Michael W. Smith,
who not only sings but cries the gospel with his life.

Contents

FOREWORD

BY MICHAEL W. SMITH

FOREWORD

From the first time I could even process anything that defined the greatness of God, I believed it.

I always knew, innately, that something bigger and better and broader than anything I could know on earth somehow controlled it all. I believed in the majesty of God before I even understood his kingdom. I believed in the goodness of God before I even really experienced it. I believed in his existence, his power, his presence, and his vastness.

But it wasn't until I discovered a little gem of a book, Brennan Manning's, *The Ragamuffin Gospel*, that an even more profound belief hit me head on: I was loved. I was in the reach of this great God who ruled the universe. I was held in the palm of the hand of the One who made everything. It's not exaggerating to say that the truths that Brennan brought to life in that book brought me back to life. For the first time I actually believed—no, accepted—that God loved me more completely than I could ever imagine.

Night after night for the past year I have had the privilege of standing on a stage surrounded by great crowds of fellow witnesses as we worship the Lord together in song. And although each evening is unique and wonderful in its own way, the moment we begin the song that is the theme of this book, I am unashamedly knocked out each and every time.

He took the fall

And thought of me

Above all

The song, for me, has been a perfect coming together of the truth I knew from childhood, the wondrous revelations I discovered through the writings of Brennan Manning, and the intoxicating wonder I celebrate each time I sing "Above All." I cannot, and will not, ever get over the amazing truth that Jesus—the maker and ruler of all—stooped down just low enough to scoop me up in his arms and carry me into the fullness of his love and glory. It just does not get any better than that.

I thank God every day, not only for that most precious

gift, but for the wonderful people he's blessed to take that message to the world. Brennan Manning's words have breathed, and continue to breathe, new life into my soul. Lenny LeBlanc and Paul Baloche, the brilliant songwriters who birthed this beautiful song, inspire me to keep on singing and celebrating the miraculous truth that "Above All" reveals. And I am all the more a fortunate man who marvels each day at being blessed with the mind-blowing opportunity to use the music I love to make to take God's message to the world around me.

May this song, and this book, move you into that awe-inspiring place—the place where you, too, can discover that reckless God who set Brennan Manning's life on fire. Who loves every one of us no matter where we've been or what we've done. And who thinks of you and me and places us in his very own heart . . . above all.

MICHAEL W. SMITH

INTRODUCTION

ABOVE ALL

The Dove Award-winning song "Above All" is a moving artistic depiction of the central mystery of Christian faith, the Incarnation. In this song, the union of human and divine natures in the person of Jesus Christ is presented with stunning simplicity and unadorned poignancy. Theologically accurate and scripturally reliable, "Above All" leads the listener unobtrusively in the mystery of the dominance and centrality of Jesus in the life of the Christian and the church.

In his divinity Jesus is utterly self-contained, self-sufficient, ungraspable, and incomprehensible. The most confident theological speech and the most edifying act of worship court the danger of domesticating the whirlwind that is the Christ of God. Thirteenth-century theologian Thomas Aquinas abruptly quit writing when he realized that everything he had written was straw. How dare anyone think that he or she can predict how and why and whether the Son of God should reward or punish? Michael W. Smith sings, "Above all wisdom and all the ways of man, You were here before the world began." If Jesus were not God, he could not satisfy our thirst and taste for the infinite.

In his humanity Jesus is the Savior whose unsettling, unnerving, and unpredictable love blows like a tornado through the lives of sinful men and women. His love is beyond description, even by our best words, by the most powerful sermons we have heard and the most profound books we have ever read. The same love in the heart of Jesus as he lay dying on the cross dwells within us this moment through his transforming Spirit. When we are in conscious communion with Jesus, we are aware of the sacredness of others. Beyond society's labels, the indwelling Presence in a brother or sister makes our differences irrelevant. We meet them without needing their affirmation because we rest secure in the unrestricted love of Jesus Christ.

Awareness of Jesus is not a luxury for cloistered monks and nuns but a necessity for each of us. It profoundly affects our self-image, our relationships with others, and the manner in which we pray. Jesus said, "Make your home in me, as I make mine in you" (John 15:4).

Michael W. Smith, affectionately known as "Smitty" by his pals, is more than a gifted artist. In "Above All," the singer and the song, like the flame and the fire, are one. Infected with the love of Jesus (since only carriers can pass it on), Smitty has given to me, the master listener, his undivided attention both to my words and my silence. After a few meetings, I discovered he is like that with everyone—a humble servant of God and a trustworthy lover of people. It is with honor that I call Smitty my friend.

PART 1

ABOVE ALL THINGS

ABOVE ALL

Above all powers

Above all kings

Above all nature and all created things

Above all wisdom and all the ways of man

You were here before the world began

Above all kingdoms

Above all thrones

Above all wonders the world has ever known

Above all wealth and treasures of the earth

There's no way to measure what You're worth

CHAPTER 1

JESUS CHRIST—RULER OF ALL

"Above all nature and all created things"

Above all powers

Above all kings

Above all nature and all

created things

Above all wisdom and

all the ways of man

You were here before the world began

Jesus Christ is the Son of God and the Son of Man, the Son of David and the Son of Mary. He is the Word-made-flesh, the Incarnation of the compassion of the Father. He is Messiah, Savior, dreamer and storyteller, servant, friend, and parable of God. Close to the brokenhearted, he speaks words of comfort; he revives the crushed in spirit with words of consolation. Rescuing drunks, scalawags, and ragamuffins, he is the Shepherd who feeds, leads, and searches out.

He is prophet, poet, and troublemaker, the scourge of hypocrites and authority figures who use religion to control others, sending them sagging under great burdens of regulations, watching them stumble and refusing to offer assistance. He excoriates the perverted spirit of legalism and the smug religious bureaucrats who condemn simple folks who for good reasons have broken bad religious laws. When he looks out at the bedraggled, beat-up, bollixed, and burnt-out, his heart overflows with unspeakable tenderness.

The Christ of God proclaims good news to prostitutes and tax collectors, to those caught up in squalid choices and failed dreams. He is *Pantocrator* (ruler of all), the creator and sovereign of the cosmos, above all powers, kings, thrones, and dominations. The star Upsilon Andromedae, positioned 264 trillion miles from Planet Earth, was created through him and for him.

In the month of December, he strikes both the sacred and secular spheres of life with sledgehammer force. Suddenly, Jesus is everywhere, his presence inescapable. We may accept him or reject him, affirm him or deny him, but we cannot ignore him. Of course, he is proclaimed in speech, song, and symbol in all Christian churches. But he rides every red-nosed reindeer, lurks behind every Barbie doll, and resonates in the most desacralized "Season's Greetings." Remotely or proximately, he is toasted in every cup of Christmas cheer. Each sprig of holly is a hint of his holiness. Each cluster of mistletoe is a sign he is here.

Jesus is not merely a super-human being with an intellect keener than ours and a capacity for loving greater than ours. In the most literal sense of the word, he is *unique*. Uncreated, infinite, totally other, he surpasses and transcends all human concepts, considerations, and expectations. He is beyond anything we can intellectualize or imagine. Thus, Jesus is a scandal to men and women everywhere, because he cannot be comprehended by the rational, finite mind.

AN ENCOUNTER WITH TRANSCENDENCE

When the Korean War ended in June 1953, our United States Marine Corps company was sent to Camp Gifu, Japan, fifteen miles south of the city of Nagoya. My military operational specialty was ammunition-demolitions expert. In October we were redeployed for one month to Camp McNair near Yokohama, 250 miles north, in

In the most literal sense of the word,
Jesus is unique.
Uncreated, infinite, totally other,
he surpasses and transcends all
human concepts, considerations,
and expectations.

order to learn about recently developed military hardware.

Our train reached Yokohama at 11:00 P.M., and Marine Corps transportation got us to our destination at midnight. In the dense blackness of a moonless night, we pitched tents and crawled into our sleeping bags, comforted by news from the company commander that morning reveille would not sound until 7:00 A.M. Rising early, I grabbed my shaving kit and headed toward the latrine to take a shower. I lifted the tent flap and stepped out into the brisk morning air. No one in our platoon had stirred. I was utterly alone. The sun had just risen on Mount Fuji, and the resplendent peak was a magnificent sight.

To this day I am uncertain about what happened next—either I fainted, swooned, or had a dizzy spell. Collapsing backward, I hit my head on the still-soft ground. When I awakened fifteen or twenty seconds later, my mouth was agape and my eyes transfixed. Riveted by the shimmering, snowcapped beauty of the fourteen-thousand-foot mountain, I slowly raised myself to a sitting position. Feelings of terror and tenderness swept through my trembling body. At age nineteen, in my first-ever experience of transcendence, I kept muttering, "O God, O God!" Awe and wonder mingled with fear at the indescribable majesty and beauty of a God I did not know and who in his total otherness remained unknowable. In retrospect, this experience beyond words, speech, imagery, and conceptuality, inducing a silence deeper than the mind, was a remote preparation for my startling encounter forty years later with the luminous beauty of Jesus in his present risenness.

THE STAGGERING GRACE OF CHRIST

Through the stunning mystery of the Incarnation, this same Jesus is present to those caught in a midlife crisis, to those suffering debilitating illness or addiction, to those in the dark woods of depression, despair, and overwhelming fear. With a compassion that knows no boundary or breaking point, he startles those caught up in the love of pleasure, trapped by fierce pride, or consumed by ravenous greed with a flash of insight, suddenly revealing that their lives are a senseless, chaotic blur of misdirected energies and flawed thoughts.

The Savior, who sets us free from fear of the Father and dislike of ourselves, stirs the defeated through the painful discovery that our efforts to extricate ourselves from the shambles of our lives are self-contradictory, because the source of the shambles is our imperious ego. Huffing and puffing, scrambling for brownie points, and thrashing about trying to fix ourselves is an exercise in futility. Jesus waits and then sends a disciple to the weary soul in order to reveal the staggering meaning of grace.

Theologian Robert Barron writes, "He is the heartbroken God who heals the heartbreak of humankind. Jesus of Nazareth is the coming-together for which we have longed since Eden."

Discussing the extraordinary impact of the person of Jesus on culture and art, Barron continues: "Jesus is lovingly depicted by the Byzantine iconographers, by the artists of the catacombs, by the sculptors of the Middle

Ages, by Giotto, Leonardo, Michelangelo, Caravaggio, Rubens, Rembrandt, Manet, Picasso, and Chagall. His shadow falls on the works of Dostoevsky, Hemingway, Melville, Eliot, and Graham Greene. His cross—that strange and disturbing reminder of his terrible death—is the dominant and most recognizable symbol in the West. Jesus is, quite simply, unavoidable. Our language, behavior, attitude, perspective, our aspirations, our fears, our moral sensibility have all been indelibly marked by his mind and heart."[1]

CHAPTER 2

SEEING PAST OUR
DISTORTIONS OF JESUS
"Above all wisdom and all the ways of man"

Above all kingdoms

Above all thrones

Above all wonders the world

has ever known

own the corridors of time Christians have attempted to cope with the intimidating reality of the person of Jesus Christ. *Coping* in this sense may be defined as "our personal response of adaptation or adjustment produced by an encounter with the real Jesus."

The tendency of many Christians is to remake Jesus of Nazareth, to concoct the kind of Jesus we can live with, to project a Christ who confirms our preferences and prejudices. For example, the great English poet John Milton framed an intellectual Christ who scorned common people as "a herd confused, a miscellaneous rabble, who extol things vulgar."[1]

The inclination to construct in our own terms of reference and to reject any evidence that challenges our assumptions is human and universal. For many hippies in the sixties, Jesus was much like themselves, an agitator and social critic, a dropout from the rat race, the prophet of the counterculture. For many yuppies in the eighties, Jesus was the provider of the good life, a driven young executive with a messianic mission, the prophet of prosperity and the chauffeured limousine.

Is either the hippie Jesus or the yuppie Jesus a faithful portrait of the courageous, free, dynamic, and demanding Jesus of the New Testament?

In the musical *Godspell* we are presented with a sunshine gospel where carnivalesque humor and youthful energy entice us into a world of no personal accountability. Its selective approach gives a rollicking but essentially false idea of the gospel message. The crucifixion is an embarrassing "theological necessity" to be hastily hurdled. The resurrection is reduced to a song, "Long Live God." What do we make of a gospel that trivializes the central saving event of human history?

Historical Distortions of Jesus

In his book *Jesus Now*, Malachi Martin surveyed the historical distortions of Jesus through the ages. The first is "Jesus Caesar." In his name the church combined wealth and political power with professed service of God, an unholy marriage of church and state where the pope in his ermine cape and Caesar in silk toga banded together to build empires. We find the same specious alliance in our nation's capital today as certain religious leaders stalk the corridors of power baptizing some politicians and blacklisting others, always claiming to find support in the teaching of Jesus.

"Jesus Apollo" came later—a romantic visionary, a beautiful leader with no disturbing overtones. He became the hero of the charming and gifted gentlemen of the nineteenth and early twentieth centuries—thinkers like Henry David Thoreau and Ralph Waldo Emerson. Jesus Apollo never dirtied his hands, never walked into a migrant worker camp in Florida or a ghetto in Philadelphia. He was no Savior.

He did not advocate a living wage, decent housing, civil rights, or care for the aged.[2]

In every age and culture we tend to shape Jesus to our own image and make him over to our own needs in order to cope with the stress his unedited presence creates. "In a foxhole, Jesus is a rescue squad, in a dentist's chair a painkiller; on exam day a problem solver; in an affluent society a clean-shaven middle-of-the-roader; for a Central American guerilla a bearded revolutionary."[3]

If we think of Jesus as the friend of sinners, the sinners are likely to be our kind of people. For instance, I know that Jesus befriends alcoholics. My personal history with alcohol plus my cultural conditioning make Jesus congenial and compassionate with selective sinners just like myself. I can cope with this Jesus.

MAKING GOD IN OUR IMAGE

Blaise Pascal wrote, "God made man in his own image, and man returned the compliment." In my forty years of pastoral ministry, I have seen Christians shaping Jesus in their own image—in every case, a dreadfully small Savior. In his classic work *Your God Is Too Small*, J. B. Phillips enumerated several of the caricatures of God: Resident Policeman, Parental Hangover, Grand Old Man, Meek-and-Mild, Heavenly Bosom, Managing Director, God in a Hurry, God for the Elite, God without Godhead, and so forth.[4]

The same tendency persists in the American church today. Unwittingly, some local churches have become followers of "Jesus Torquemada." In the fifteenth century, Tomás de Torquemada and his disciples persecuted and tortured anyone who dared to disagree with their narrow interpretation of Scripture. Torquemada, whose Spanish name means "orthodoxy of doctrine," died an old man in 1498, responsible for 2,000 burnings at the stake and the exiling of 160,000 Jews from Spain as undesirable aliens—all for the glory of God.[5]

Contemporary Torquemadas flourish in many Christian denominations and nondenominations.

In every age and culture we tend to
shape Jesus to our own image
and make him over to our own needs
in order to cope with the stress
his unedited presence creates.

Their underlying premise is: "There is no salvation outside my church." Like Torquemada, they exhibit small-mindedness and ostracism of those who dare to challenge their nonhistorical orthodoxy. Religion has petrified their compassion.

They may reflect a strict sexual morality and turn a blind eye to the helpless, the needy, the victimized, and the distressed. Within their communities flourishes a hyperspiritualized version of salvation that is intensely concerned with self. To all appearances, such a salvation ferments in the mind only, a kind of pseudo-ecstasy, without cost or empathy or a sense of the suffering of the innocent. Little concerned to dialogue with other churches, self-exempted from the judgment of God, they are indifferent to the plight of the poor but much concerned with something known as the "afterlife." Confined in the coffin of their own orthodoxy, such churches bring only discord and division to the body of Christ.

Other churches go through the motions of this or

that desultory or raucous liturgy or worship. As Daniel Berrigan notes, "Hearts are elsewhere, words void, gestures all of appeasement, of bad faith. Perhaps this God of ours can be cajoled, persuaded to stand with us, with our armies, our gross national product, our pentagon, our world markets. . . . Perhaps this God is amenable to fine words, songs, gestures, coins raining down, grandiloquent art and architecture. Perhaps Yahweh is like us, a God tut-tutting our little weaknesses. Perhaps our God can be hoodwinked."[6]

THE REAL JESUS

Jesus Christ, in whom the fullness of divinity dwells, is not to be boxed, tamed, defined, interred or disinterred, made plausible or comprehensible, explained or explained away, reduced to polemic, located within or beyond creation, liberated or captivated, housebroken or templebroken.

As Michael W. Smith sings, Jesus is "Above all powers, above all kings, above all nature and all created things. Above all wisdom and all the ways of man, [he was] here before the world began."

Jesus is beyond language, enticement, placation, invocation, use or misuse. He is beyond our wild desire or inertia, our hope or hopelessness, our rectitude or wickedness. He cannot be cornered by sweet talk, by gentle persuasion, or by a bribe. Neither is he to be reduced to a plaything, a caged songbird for the amusement of children.

Christian history offers ample testimony that we have contrived a god who resembles ourselves, a mirror image of appetite, fanaticism, financial profit, political muscle, bloodline, nationality, or whatever our passing fancy, and we have worshiped this god of human manufacturing, a god who does not exist. Likewise, the god whose moods alternate between graciousness and fierce anger, the god who is tender when we are good and relentlessly punishing when we are bad, the god who exacts the last drop of blood from his Son so that his just anger, evoked by sin, may be appeased, is not the God revealed by and in Jesus Christ. And if he is not the God of Jesus, he does not exist.

The contemporary distortions and caricatures of God that litter the Christian landscape—ranging from the inflamed, splenetic deity who sanctions the slaughter of innocent people (9-11) because homosexuals and abortionists have provoked his murderous wrath, to the benign, permissive patriarch who winks at adultery, countenances bigotry, and shrugs when hoodwinked Christians finally flee the church to preserve their faith and their sanity—are the handiwork of successful salesmen posing as spiritual leaders.

These aberrations also make us profoundly grateful for the church's firm and fast identification of Jesus as the Christ, the Son of the living God, who refuses to be contaminated by the fads and fantasies of power brokers, lunatic liberals, and right-wing extremists.

Jesus Christ, in whom the fullness
of divinity dwells, is not to be
boxed, tamed, defined, interred or
disinterred, made plausible or
comprehensible, explained or explained away,
liberated or captivated,
housebroken or templebroken.

CHAPTER 3

THE INFINITE AND INTIMATE CHRIST

"There's no way to measure what You're worth"

Above all wealth and treasures

of the earth

There's no way to measure

what You're worth

THREE

Who is the real Jesus inscribed on the pages of the four Gospels?

The Gospel writers present Jesus as *above* ("In the beginning was the Word: the Word was with God and the Word was God" [John 1:1]) and *below* (he experiences fatigue and indecision. He is heartbroken at the death of his friend Lazarus. He performs a miracle at Cana of Galilee for the pleasure of it. He drinks his people's wine, sings their wedding songs, and is accused of being a drunkard and a glutton). He is transcendent and immanent, infinite and more intimate to us than we are to ourselves.

As Luke Timothy Johnson notes, "The four canonical gospels are remarkably consistent on one essential aspect of the identity and mission of Jesus. Their fundamental focus is not on Jesus' wondrous works nor on his wise words. Their shared focus is on the *character* of his life and death. They all reveal the same *pattern* of radical obedience to God and selfless love toward people. All four Gospels also agree that discipleship is to follow the same *messianic pattern*. They do not emphasize the performance of certain deeds or the learning of certain doctrines. They insist on living the same pattern of life and death shown by Jesus."[1]

The letters of the apostle Paul remind us that we are to live according to the mind of Christ. Following the real Jesus is not a matter of working wonders, of becoming a famous preacher or writer, of creating a huge church or becoming a charismatic leader. It is instead a matter of transformation according to the pattern of the Messiah. The "real Jesus" is therefore the sovereign Lord who through the Holy Spirit replicates in the lives of believers faithful obedience to God by loving service to our brothers and sisters in the human family.

The Jesus who sits at the right hand of the Father is the same Jesus who washes the feet of the apostles. (The dress and duty are those of a slave.) The ruler of the universe is the same Jesus who asks the plaintive question, "Simon, son of John, do you love me more than these others do?" (John 21:15). The only begotten Son of the Father is the same heartbroken Christ who weeps over Jerusalem. The Lord of glory is the same Jesus who dwells within us: "Make your home in me, as I make mine in you" (John 15:4).

JESUS' RELATIONSHIP TO OTHERS

The relational spirit of Jesus with family, friends, sinners, and ragamuffins was beautifully expressed to me on a tour through Sleepy Hollow Village on the Hudson River in New York. Our guide's only instruction was, "Please be gentle with the lambs. They won't come to you if you frighten them."

Jesus did not beat up on broken people. When his eyes scanned the streets and hillsides, he felt sorry because the people were leaderless. He never belittled, shamed, or ridiculed them. He took the initiative in seeking out the lost and wayward and did not attempt to convert them with one shattering blow after another of the Torah and the Hebrew prophets. His mind was constantly infused with mercy, tenderness, and forgiveness. He did not lecture the woman caught in adultery on the consequences of future infidelity; he saw her dignity being destroyed by so-called religious men. After reminding them of their solidarity in sinfulness, he *looked* at the woman with eyes of immense tenderness, forgave her, and told her not to sin anymore. This moment, you and I are being seen with the same gaze of infinite tenderness.

In the synoptic Gospels (Matthew, Mark, and Luke), Jesus places the love of one's neighbor on the same level of obligation as the love of God. Matthew 25:31-46 seems to make the entire judgment of personal worth, of human success and failure, depend on how one has responded to human need. The love of others is neither sentiment nor abstraction. The issue is not how we feel about our neighbor but what we have done for him or her. Of course, Jesus reduced all of the Law, meaning all moral obligations, to the one obligation of loving God and the least brother and sister, near and far.

To be loved means to be *looked* at in such a manner that the reality of recognition is disclosed. The Christian who looks at—rather than merely sees—another, communicates to the one looked at that he or she is being recognized as a subject in an impersonal world of objects, a person and not merely a function, as *someone* and not everyone. This issue lies at the very grassroots of justice: to recognize the other as a human being with the image of God flowing on his or her brow.

The mere purchase of a postage stamp or a load of groceries can occasion an exchange of glances between clerk and customer that is capable of transforming a routine gesture into an authentic encounter that is mutually ennobling. On the way out the door, if the customer looks over his shoulder, he should not be surprised to see the clerk smiling at the next customer.

The fundamental secret of Jesus in relationship to others was his sovereign respect for their dignity. They were not toys, emoluments, functions, or occasions for personal compensation. In Luke's account of the passion and death of Jesus, the evangelist notes that after Peter's third denial, Jesus turned and *looked* at Peter. In that look the reality of recognition was disclosed. Peter knew that no one had ever loved him as Jesus did. Christ looked at the man who had confessed him as the Christ, the Son of the living God, watched him act out the dreadful drama of his addiction to personal safety, and loved him. The love of Christ for Peter lay in his complete and unconditional acceptance of him in his cowardice.

In his reaction to Peter, no man in human history was freer, more independent of pressures, conventions, and expectations. Jesus was so liberated from the consciousness-dominating barrage of desires, demands, and inflexible emotional programming that he could accept the unacceptable. Jesus had been betrayed, but he did not resort to vicious attacks or terrifying threats. He communicated his deepest feelings to the apostle by a single look! And that look transformed Peter: "He went outside and wept bitterly" (Luke 22:62).

REVERSING THE RULES

When Jesus tied a towel around his waist, poured water into a copper basin, and washed the dirty feet of the apostles, the Maundy Thursday revolution began. An unprecedented idea of greatness in the kingdom of God emerged: The disciple who humbles himself, seeks the last place, and becomes like a little child is exalted.

What a shocking reversal of our culture's priorities and values! To prefer to be the servant rather than the lord of the household, to merrily taunt the gods of prestige, power, and recognition, to refuse to take

The fundamental secret of Jesus in
relationship to others was his
sovereign respect for their dignity.
This issue lies at the very grassroots
of justice: to recognize the other as
a human being with the image
of God flowing on his or her brow.

oneself seriously, to live without gloom by a lackey's agenda—these are the attitudes and actions that bear the stamp of authentic discipleship. In effect, Jesus said, "Blessed are you if you love to be unknown and regarded as nothing." All things being equal, to prefer contempt to honor, to prefer ridicule to praise, to prefer humiliation to glory—these are formulas of greatness in the new Israel of God.

Jesus Christ is above all, as he becomes the least of all. "His state was divine, yet he did not cling to his equality with God but emptied himself to assume the condition of a slave, and became as men are; and being as all men are, he was humbler yet, even to accepting death, death on a cross" (Philippians 2:6–8).

Jesus' ministry of service is rooted in his compassion for the lost, lonely, and broken. Why does he love losers, failures, and those on the margin of social respectability? Because the Father does. "I tell you most solemnly, the Son can do nothing by himself; he can do only what he sees the Father doing: and whatever the Father does the Son does too" (John 5:19).

In Jesus of Nazareth, the mind of God becomes transparent. There is nothing of self to be seen, only the passionate, pursuing love of God. Jesus lays bare the heart of God through his life of humble service. In fact, when Jesus returns, it will not be with the impact of unbearable glory; he will come as a servant. "Happy those servants whom the master finds awake when he comes. I tell you solemnly, he will put on an apron, sit them down at table and wait on them" (Luke 12:37).

Since the day that Jesus burst the bonds of death and the messianic era erupted into history, there is a new agenda, a unique set of priorities, and a revolutionary hierarchy of values. The Nazarene carpenter did not simply refine Platonic and Aristotelian ethics; he did not merely reorder Old Testament spirituality; he did not simply reorder the old creation. He brought a nonviolent revolution. We must renounce all that we possess, not just most of it (Luke 14:33); we must give up our old way of life, not merely correct some aberrations in it (Ephesians 4:22); we are to be an altogether new creation, not simply a refurbished version of the old self (Galatians 6:15); we are to be transformed from one glory to another, even into the very image of Jesus, utterly transparent (2 Corinthians 3:18); our minds are to be renewed by a spiritual revolution (Ephesians 4:23).

Why? So that we may be free to love one another in the same selfless way that Jesus loves us, and to walk daily in faithful, obedient love, as the real Jesus did.

JESUS CHRIST—BEYOND AND WITHIN

Jesus Christ is beyond and within our human experience of life and love. *Beyond*, as Son of God and Second Person of the holy and undivided Trinity, he cannot be imagined, since God cannot be imagined. Therefore, we cannot know him as he really is unless we pass beyond everything that can be imagined and pass into an obscurity without images and without the likeness of any created thing.

Within, Jesus is an indwelling presence. Is this our real sin—the unawareness of his immediate presence? Jesus is our brother, friend, servant, lover, countercultural Christ, and life-giving Spirit. The real Jesus forms, informs, and transforms his followers through the gift of the Holy Spirit, who organizes our lives and generates our activities.

Since I began writing this little book, one question continues to disquiet me: What does the Christian life look like, once one is smitten by the love of Jesus Christ?

Since the day that Jesus burst
the bonds of death and the
messianic era erupted into history,
there is a new agenda,
a unique set of priorities, and a
revolutionary heirarchy of values.

PART 2

YOU THOUGHT OF ME
ABOVE ALL

Crucified

Laid behind the stone

You lived to die

Rejected and alone

Like a rose

Trampled on the ground

You took the fall

And thought of me

Above all

CHAPTER 4

LOVE AFFAIR WITH THE
CRUCIFIED SAVIOR

"Crucified, laid behind the stone"

Crucified

Laid behind the stone

You lived to die

At age twenty-one, I entered seminary. After three years in the Marine Corps and a semester at the University of Missouri, where I was preparing to enter the School of Journalism, life suddenly seemed empty. One October night in 1955, I had a dream that blew my secure, well-regulated, and spiritually impoverished life apart.

In my dream, I was driving a powder blue Cadillac convertible up a steep hill, and the scene seemed more real than reality. At the crest of the hill was a fourteen-room ranch-style house affording a panoramic view of the valley below. My name was on the mailbox. Parked in the circular driveway was my wife's car, a Porsche. Inside the house Barbara was baking bread and the voices of our four kids rang out to greet me. I looked in the rearview mirror and decided that my white hair needed a trim. I was about fifty years old. As I opened the front door, I glanced at the gold-trimmed plaque on the wall—the Nobel Prize for literature awarded to me.

I woke up in a cold sweat bellowing, "O God, there has to be more! Am I going to invest the next thirty years of my life to achieve, fame, wealth, and success only to suddenly discover that's all there is?"

An appalling restlessness swept over me, accompanied by a nagging sense of personal dissatisfaction. *What's wrong with receiving the rewards that society bestows on gifted people? Why can't I be content with a life that many people covet? How can this "more" be so pressing and urgent when I don't know what the "more" is?* Yet I knew there was no turning back until I found out what it was. Unsettled and confused, I embarked on the search for what proved to be Jesus.

THE FURIOUS LOVE OF CHRIST

After seven days in seminary, I realized that the parched, dismal journey to the ordained priesthood was not for me—rising at 5:00 A.M., chanting psalms in Latin with pantywaist eighteen-year-old postulants, ordered to eat beets (which I hated), and stumbling up steps in an ankle-length robe unaware that I had to lift the hem. I endured seven days solely because my brother Rob had bet me fifty bucks that I would not last a week.

On the morning of the eighth day, with my bags packed and my spirit soaring, I went to inform the local superior that I was leaving. He was not in his office. To kill time, I went to the chapel to say good-bye to God and thank him for my escape from the rigors of religious life. Not one to shun the heroic, I decided to do something great for God. Even though it was not required, I would walk the fourteen "stations of the cross," a spiritual devotion focused on the passion and death of Jesus Christ.

Unable to pray without the help of a book, I grabbed a leaflet. At the first station, "Jesus is condemned to death," I read the prayer rapidly, made a hasty genuflection like I'd smelled smoke in the building, and hurried on to station number two.

I woke up in a cold sweat bellowing,
"O God, there has to be more!
Am I going to invest the next thirty
years of my life to achieve
fame, wealth, and success only to discover
that's all there is?"

After eleven minutes of reading prayers and touching one knee to the floor, I arrived at the twelfth station, "Jesus dies on the cross." The rubric in the leaflet instructed worshipers to kneel. As I sank to my knees, the Angelus bell from the cloistered Carmelite monastery a half-mile away sounded in the distance. It was exactly noon. At fine minutes after three, I rose from my knees sensing that the most thrilling adventure of my life had just begun.

At the outset of the three hours, I felt like a little boy kneeling at the seashore. Little waves washed in and lapped at my knees. Slowly the waves got bigger until they reached my waist. Suddenly a tremendous wave of concussion force knocked me over and swept me off the beach. Reeling in midair, arching through space, I intuited that I was not only airborne but being carried to a place I had never been before—the heart of Jesus Christ.

When he called my name, it was not Richard, my baptismal name, or Brennan, but another word that I shall not disclose, a word that is my real name in the mind of God, a name spoken with indescribable tenderness and written on the white stone (Revelation 2:17).

In my first-ever experience of being loved for nothing I had done or could do, I moved back and forth between mild ecstasy, silent wonder, and hushed trembling. The aura might be best described as "bright darkness." The moment lingered on in a timeless now, until without warning I felt a hand grip my heart. It was abrupt and startling.

The awareness of being loved was no longer tender and comforting. The love of Christ, the crucified Son of God, took on the wild fury of a sudden spring storm. Like a dam bursting, a spasm of convulsive crying erupted from the depths of my soul. *Jesus died on the cross for me.* I had known that since grade school, in the way of what John Henry Newman called "notional knowledge"—abstract, far away, irrelevant to the gut issues of life, another trinket in the dusty pawnshop of doctrinal beliefs. But in one blinding moment of salvific truth, it became real knowledge calling for personal engagement of my heart. Christianity was no longer merely a moral code, an ethic, or a philosophy of life but a love affair.

At last, drained, spent, and lost in speechless humility, I was back kneeling at the seashore with gentle waves of love sweeping over me, saturating my mind and heart in a quiet, unselfconscious mode of silent adoration.

At 3:05 P.M. I rose shakily from the floor and returned to my room. Resonating with amazement and affectionate awe, I entered a new mode of existence wherein "There is only Christ: he is everything and he is in everything" (Colossians 3:11).[1]

OUR RESPONSE TO CHRIST'S LOVE

The chorus of "Above All"—"You took the fall and thought of me above all"—transmogrifies the memory of February 8, 1956, into a present, ongoing reality. As Bernard of Clairvaux wrote in his eleventh-century treatise on the love of God, "Only one who has experienced it can begin to understand what the love of Christ truly is."[2]

Our response to Jesus will be total the day we experience how total is his love for us. Instead of our self-conscious efforts to be good, we should allow ourselves the luxury of letting ourselves be loved, not after we clean up our act and get all our ducks in a row, not after we have eliminated every trace of sin, selfishness, dishonesty, and degraded love from our résumé, not after we have developed a disciplined prayer life and spent ten years in Calcutta with Mother Teresa's missionaries, but right now, right here, holding this book in your hands.

*In one blinding moment of salvific
truth, Christianity became
no longer merely a moral code, an ethic,
or a philosophy of life,
but a love affair.*

CHAPTER 5

OUR CONFIDENCE THROUGH
CHRIST'S HUMILIATION
"You lived to die, rejected and alone"

Rejected and alone

Like a rose

trampled on the ground

FIVE

I f the demons' main work is deception, Good
Friday was triumphant high noon for the
father of lies. The crowd, incited by the chief
priests, demanded the freedom of Barabbas from
Pontius Plate, the visibly anxious procurator of Rome.

The crowd was quickly becoming not only impossible but dangerous. Pilate could not allow that to happen. The truth about him was revealed in his life of compromise, in his willingness, when the chips were down, to save himself by doing what he must do. Satan's pawn was a politician forced to live by the version of truth that worked.

The wily work of the evil one continues in the world today through maneuvers such as the monstrous atrocity of 9-11 for allegedly religious reasons, but he moves in subtler ways within the Christian community today. Like a shrewd enemy commander, Satan circles the ramparts of our personality to determine where we are most vulnerable. He knows that blatant temptations like murder, theft, adultery, and character assassination would be instantly recognized and dispatched. Therefore, he insinuates himself into that part of our psyche were we are most vulnerable. For example, he seduces us into dwelling on our past sins and stirs the pot of self-hatred. Although these sins have been forgiven and forgotten by God, the father of lies first robs us of the peace and joy of the Holy Spirit.

Tormented by sins that no longer exist in the inner reaches of eternity, we focus on memories of our lust, greed, arrogance, missed opportunities, broken marriages, estranged children, or pain inflicted on family, friends, or colleagues, and in high dudgeon we lacerate ourselves for real and even imagined failures.

THE DECEPTION OF DENIGRATION

Low self-esteem and a negative self-image would not

be so damaging, save for the fact that they condition our perception of the world and our interaction with others in terms consistent with our self-concept. Viewing ourselves as basically unlovable, we negate our own worth, are plagued by feelings of insecurity, inadequacy, and inferiority, and are closed to the value of others because they threaten our very existence. We perceive the exaltation of another as a personal attack and respond in kind.

Fear is manifested by the feeling that we do not belong. In our self-talk we say in effect, "I am a loser; I am in the way; nobody cares." In group gatherings we feel like intruders. "Nobody loves me; everybody hates me; I shouldn't be here." In a simple conversation with significant others, their lack of enthusiasm confirms what we already suspected: "I am a bore." We pass a friend on the street. Distracted, he ignores us, and we are crushed. When we put our heads on the pillow at night, we ignore the pleasant aspects on the day to fasten on the fleeting incidents that reflect our negative self-portrait.

Like a shrewd enemy commander,
Satan circles the ramparts of
our personality to determine where
we are most vulnerable,
and insinuates himself into
that part of our psyche.

The Christian with a poor self-image, deceived by Lucifer, is reluctant to take risks. In a classroom, Bible study, or an evening with friends, she never asks a question. If she stays silent, the group (she hopes) may assume she is a profound thinker. Rather than risk a negative evaluation—"What a stupid question!"—she feels that it is safer to say nothing, wear an intelligent mask, and let the group suspect she is brilliant. Needless to say, she experiences great anxiety over her mistakes.

Our tendency to berate ourselves for real or imagined failures, to belittle ourselves and savage our self-worth, to dwell exclusively on our dishonesty, self-centeredness, and lack of personal discipline is the hegemony of low self-esteem, spawned by Satan.

Where is the crucified Jesus who bore our infirmities and carried all our sins in this self-destructive situation? In his keynote address in Atlantic City, Francis MacNutt touched an exposed nerve when he thundered, "If the crucified Christ has washed you in his own blood and forgiven you all your sins, what right do you have not to forgive yourself?"

Beware the evil one who prowls the earth seeking to undo what God has done in the passion and death of Jesus Christ! As I write these words and you read them, the incomparable love of Jesus is a maelstrom flashing like lightning across our lives.

To escape our demons we seek comfort in our addictions: alcohol or being right, workaholism or winning, ice cream, television, religion, cocaine, movies, marijuana, money, power, sex, gambling, compulsive reading, or simply having the last word. What is conspicuously missing is an unshaken trust in the merciful love of the crucified, redeeming Christ.

A story is told of three monks who were praying in their abbey. One monk felt himself rising out of his body. As he moved closer to heaven, he could see the other two monks seated in the pews beneath him. One was taken in reverie as he began to hear his praises sung by choirs of angels. The remaining monk was filled with distractions and could only think of how long it had been since he had eaten a Big Mac. Later that night the devil's assistant was reporting on the day's activities. "I was working on three monks who were praying in their church," he said, "but I was successful in tempting only two of them."[1]

THE SEDUCTION OF SEPARATING SPIRITUAL FROM SECULAR

The Liar works effectively within us when we attempt to separate the spiritual life from ordinary life, when we divide fixed times of personal prayer and communal worship from cleaning, raising children, carpooling, working indoors or outdoors, walking, playing, or biting into a Big Mac.

When I read the local newspaper or *Sports Illustrated*, a mystery novel by P. D. James or Elizabeth George, is this recreation unspiritual but reading Oswald Chambers or Philip Yancey spiritual? Is God absent when I play Scrabble, get a haircut, toss a

Frisbee, make love, vote, walk the dog, see a movie, make a living, wash the car, or bury my nose in a pint of Ben & Jerry's? While baking a cake, do I have to listen to a tape of Gordon MacDonald to feel that I am pleasing God? The apparent dichotomy, engineered by the prince of darkness, between the spiritual life and the quotidian, often mundane activities that constitute the woof and warp of life banish Jesus within us to the savannahs of heaven. The journey becomes prosaic rather than poetic, speech rather than song, and tangibles, visibles, and perishables become an adequate substitute for Paul's ringing affirmation, "Life to me . . . is Christ" (Philippians 1:21).

FREE TO ACCEPT CHRIST'S LOVE

A poet has written that the last illusion we must let go of is the desire to feel loved. The evil one prompts us to attach great importance to prayer experiences filled with an intense awareness of God's presence and to denigrate times when we feel nothing, are continually

distracted, and struggling with temptations. The idea
that God is simply delighted when we show up and shut
up does not cross our minds.

When a veteran monk was asked, "Do you feel
closer to God now than when you entered the monastery
thirty years ago?" his glorious answer was, "No, but now
it doesn't matter." Freed from the necessity of feeling
loved, he was able to accept consolation or desolation
indiscriminately because of his unwavering trust in the
Presence in season and out of season.

Beware the evil one who prowls about the
church seeking to undo what God has done in the
passion and death of Jesus Christ! He seeks to oblit-
erate our self-worth, to obscure our core identity as
the beloved children of God, and to deny the
Incarnation by separating our life in the Spirit from
our life in the world of everyday.

Beware the evil one who prowls the earth
seeking to undo what God has
done in the passion and death of Jesus Christ!
As I write these words and you read,
the incomparable love of Jesus is a maelstrom
flashing like lightning across our lives.

CHAPTER 6

THE TRANSFORMING PRESENCE
OF THE RISEN LORD

"You took the fall and thought of me above all"

You took the fall

and thought of me

Above all

The risen Jesus is identifiable only as the crucified one with the brilliant wounds of his Good Friday battle shining in his hands, feet, and side. In his present risenness, Jesus remains the Man of the cross.

Of course, the song "Above All" is nonsense and every book written about Jesus is senseless, if Christ is not risen. If Easter is not history, we must become cynics. We either look upon the death of Jesus on the cross as the ultimate defeat of a good man by the powers of darkness or we cast our lot and our lives with a new power that has been unleashed in the world. If Jesus had not returned from the grave, he would be, as Albert Schweitzer memorably put it, one more person ground under the wheel of history.

The apostle Paul writes, "If Christ has not been raised then our preaching is useless and your believing it is useless. . . . If our hope in Christ has been for this life only, we are the most unfortunate of all people" (1 Corinthians 15:13, 19). The early Christians were galvanized by their invincible conviction that the one who was hung on a tree was not entombed, but raised up by the Father.

In light of this Easter faith in the risen Jesus, the cross is seen not as a tragic ending to a noble life but as a revelation of God's heart. Barron writes, "The terrible rivalry, the Promethean struggle, the awful illusion that God is a threatening human being, all of it is shattered, broken through, by the cross and resurrection of Christ."[1]

The Friday we call Good and the Sunday celebrating Easter are the supreme manifestations of God's love for us. Jesus' breakthrough from death to life declares that the Abba of Jesus has not consigned his Son *and* us to the dustbin of history. Death is tripped of its dark power; it is a phantom, the bogeyman of little children;

its purpose is to usher us into the one experience worthy of the name "life." Jesus could have saved us with the simple wave his of hand and said, "All your sins are forgiven." But would we have ever come to know the depths of God's love without the slaughtered Son now raised on high?

THE FOUNDATION OF OUR FAITH

It is invaluable to remember that the Gospels were not available to the earliest Christians. Scholarly consensus dates the first written Gospel of Mark to between the years 68–73 of the Christian era. The first and earliest letter of Paul to the Thessalonians is traced to 50–51 C.E. Since the New Testament had not yet been written, the obvious question arises: What was the foundation of the earliest Christians' faith?

ORAL TRADITION

The first increment in the foundation of the early Christians' faith was the oral tradition (from the Latin

Underestimate the love of the crucified
and risen Jesus, and
the shadow of shame, guilt,
and fear darkens our space without respite.

tradere, meaning "to hand over") from the apostles. The eyewitnesses of the empty tomb and the various appearances of the risen Jesus proclaimed fearlessly the good news: "God raised this man Jesus to life, and all of us are witnesses to that" (Acts 2:32). Peter, John, Philip, James, and the others, once hiding in the Upper Room "for fear of the Jews," were empowered by the Holy Spirit not only to proclaim but, with the exception of John, to gladly suffer martyrdom for the sake of Jesus.

After the two disciples on the road to Emmaus told their story to the Eleven, Jesus himself "stood among them and said to them, 'Peace be with you.' In a state of alarm and fright, they thought they were seeing a ghost. But he said, 'Why are you so agitated, and why are these doubts rising in your hearts? Look at my hands and feet; yes, it is I indeed. Touch me and see for yourselves; a ghost has no flesh and bones as you can see I have.' And as he said this he showed them his hands and feet. Their joy was so great that they still could not believe it, and they stood there dumbfounded" (Luke 24:36–41).

Why were the apostles "in a state of alarm and fright"? Why were they scared out of their wits, so full of fear? For the very same reason I would be—guilt!

Certainly the extraordinary phenomenon of the man who was crucified standing before them in radiant health made them think they were seeing a ghost, and that may be the primary cause of their fear. What is the central theme of most ghost stories? The genre usually features an innocent victim of foul play who is killed and resuscitated to life, angrily seeking bloodthirsty revenge. In the boundary moment of Jesus' life, when the sentence of death by crucifixion was mandated, where were his loyal followers? Judas betrayed him, Peter denied him, and the rest abandoned him.

Are the disciples wondering if Jesus is bent on retribution? Are they terrified because they think Jesus has returned for payback, to remind them of their cowardice and infidelity and settle accounts once and for all? Guilt and fear, alarm and fright would not be inappropriate emotions given all that has occurred. If their hearts trembled, so would mine.

I shall not mince words. Although alcoholism is a disease, it is also a life of utter selfishness, or as the Big Book of AA states, "Self will run riot." It was not merely a matter of drinking too much; the fabric of my moral life deteriorated to the point that I broke every one of the Ten Commandments. Inflicting pain and heartache on family and friends, unavailable to help anyone in need, I missed my own mother's funeral because I was drunk. My indifference to Jesus and callous disregard of his people is a chapter of shame in my life that makes identification with the guilty and fearful apostles not merely a pious thought but a flagrant, poignant reality.

Underestimate the love of the crucified and risen Jesus, and the shadow of shame, guilt, and fear darkens our space without respite. Dismiss the chorus of the song—"You took the fall and thought of me above all"—as wishful thinking or fiction, and the love of the redeeming Christ is excluded from our Christian purview. I write these words not as a spectator but as an active participant in a lifelong struggle with self-hatred that ended only when I let myself be loved in my brokenness.

On Easter night when Jesus appears to the Eleven who betrayed, denied, and ran out on him, he seems to have no memory of their infamy. Without a trace of rage or righteous indignation, he speaks the simple word "peace." The same ineffable experience of freedom from guilt and peace of heart is offered by Jesus, who is "the same today as he was yesterday and as he will be for ever" (Hebrews 13:8), to anyone who risks letting him run wild in their lives.

PERSONAL EXPERIENCE

The second increment in the foundation of the early Christians' faith was their personal experience of the present risenness of Jesus. They felt Christ actively present in their lives. The resurrection was both a historically past event in a specific time and place and an

*If the historical Jesus
initiated the Way that will forever
identify his true disciples,
the resurrected Christ
animates the lives of his followers.*

ongoing reality impacting their lives in the here and now. A power greater than themselves, released by the Easter Jesus through the Spirit of Pentecost, was dynamically operative in their lives.

The first Christians were not supermen and superwomen miraculously inoculated against envy, sloth, and selfishness in its myriad forms. Like the rest of us, they struggled mightily with what C. S. Lewis called "a zoo of lusts, a bedlam of ambitions, a nursery of fears, a harem of fondled hatreds."[2] Having inherited the originating sin of Adam, they were prey to the same dangers, difficulties, and temptations that threaten to pull us down.

The abiding presence of the risen Jesus was not a chimera for the post-Easter Christians. If the historical Jesus initiated the Way that will forever identify his true disciples, the resurrected Christ animates the lives of his followers. This is the existential experience of the faith community before the New Testament evolved into its written form. Jesus Christ had not only entered human history but now, transhistorically through the Holy Spirit, he lives in his disciples. Through this divine empowerment, things that were impossible are now possible. His followers can now live the same kind of life as Christ lived (1 John 2:6), do as he did (John 13:15), love as he loved (Ephesians 5:2), forgive as he forgave (Colossians 3:13), and in their minds "be the same as Christ Jesus" (Philippians 2:5). Therefore they are able to follow Christ's example (1 Peter 2:21), lay down their lives for the brethren as he did (John 3:16), and claim with Paul, "I live now not with my own life but with the life of Christ who lives in me" (Galatians 2:20).

Our tragic mistake today is to minimize "how infinitely great is power that he has exercised for us believers" (Ephesians 1:19)—*the same power* he used in raising Christ from the dead! To settle for mediocrity, to surrender to our addictions, to capitulate to the world, and to resign ourselves to a humdrum life of hoeing cabbage and drinking beer is to nullify the power of the crucified, resurrected Jesus and the total sufficiency of his redeeming work.

The Christ in us is not only our hope for future glory but a transforming presence within who promises, "Whoever believes in me will perform the same works as I do myself, he will perform even greater works" (John 14:12).

THE JOY OF CHRIST'S RESURRECTION

Mother Teresa chose to live her life among the most afflicted human beings on earth. Yet she could say, "Never let anything so fill you with sorrow as to make you forget the joy of Christ risen."[3]

Jesus Christ risen from the dead is the source, reason, and basis for the inarticulate joy of Christian living. He is the Lord of the dance—the dance of the living. He is the Lord of laughter, and our laughter is the echo of his risen life within us. On Easter Monday, Orthodox monks sit in the monastery all day telling jokes and laughing till their sides hurt.

It is the risen Lord of glory who says to us with sovereign authority, "Blessed are you who laugh now because you can bring the joy of Easter to others. Blessed are you if you can laugh at yourselves, refuse to take yourselves seriously, and not allow your heartaches and hiatal hernias to become the center of your lives.

"Blessed are you if you can take delight in all of my Father's creation: in sun and surf, snow and star, in blue marlin and robin redbreast, in Paul Cezanne, Olivia Newton-John, veal scallopini, the love of a man or woman, and the presence of the Holy Spirit within you. Blessed are you if you have let go of all that shackles you to yesterday, imprisons you in your small self today, and frightens you with the uncertainty of tomorrow. Blessed are you who laugh now because you are free!"

Jesus Christ risen from the dead
is the Lord of the dance—the dance of the living.
He is the Lord of laughter, and our laughter
is the echo of his risen life within us.

NOTES

CHAPTER 1: JESUS CHRIST—RULER OF ALL

1. Robert Barron, *That I May See: A Theology of Transformation* (New York: Crossroad Publishing, 1998), 159–60.

CHAPTER 2: SEEING PAST OUR DISTORTIONS OF JESUS

1. John Milton, *Paradise Regained*, Book Three, lines 49–51.
2. Malachi Martin, *Jesus Now* (New York: E. P. Dutton,1973).
3. Walter J. Burghardt, *Still Proclaiming Your Wonders* (New York: Paulist Press, 1984), 140.
4. J. B. Phillips, *Your God Is Too Small* (New York: Macmillan, 1987, reissue ed.).
5. Excerpted from Brennan Manning, *The Signature of Jesus* (Sisters, Ore.: Multnomah, 1996, revised ed.), 159–62.
6. Daniel Berrigan, *Isaiah: Spirit of Courage, Gift of Tears* (Minneapolis: Fortress Press, 1996), 33–34.

CHAPTER 3: THE INFINITE AND INTIMATE CHRIST

1. Luke Timothy Johnson, *The Real Jesus* (San Francisco: HarperSanFrancisco, 1996), 157–58.